FACTORS RESPONSIBLE FOR STRESS AMONG WORKING CLASS MARRIED WOMEN HEALTH CARE PERSONNEL

By

Chuks Ojieh

TABLE OF CONTENTS

ABSTRACT

I carried out to investigate factors responsible for stress among working class married women in a hospital using Cornerstone Hospital. A hundred self-administered questionnaires was distributed to randomly select married women working in the hospital comprising 13 doctors, 26 nurses, 8 Pharmacists, 26 administrative staff, 7 medical laboratory personnel, 6 from medical records, 3 form catering department and 11 health attendants. The major and common source of stress pressure points, found in this study include having too much work to do, coping with office politics, supervision of the work of others and having responsibility for same. Other stressors observed also include presence of role ambiguity in nature of work, having to keep up with advances in technology and demand made by work on private/social life. Worrying about hospital's culpability to customers is another source of stress as well as working shifts. (This is prominent for doctors, nurses, catering and medical laboratory staff. Hypothesis testing using X^2-square shows that there is significant difference in stress experienced by married women working different schedules in hospital (Hypothesis one). Hypothesis three likewise revealed significant difference in stress and years of working experience at present job. Hypothesis two revealed that there is no significant difference in stress experienced and age.

CHAPTER ONE

DEFINITION OF STRESS

Stress is a feeling of tension or pressure, experienced when the demands placed on them exceed the resources has in order to meet demands.

Stress is aptly called "DISEASE OF CIVILIZATION OR INVISIBLE DISEASE". It is a pattern specific and non-specific responses an organism makes to stimulus events that disturb its equilibrium or exceed one's ability to cope.

According to Sely 1976, stress is a state within an organism characterized by general adaptation syndrome (GAS). In other word, it is the non-specific response of the body to the demands made upon it. It suggests excessive demand that produce disturbance of physical, sociological and psychological systems (Albar and Gorcia 2005). Stress has effect on every facet of human life which may be acute or chronic in nature (Akinboye and Ekunjimi 2002). It exists in different forms. It may be psychological, emotional, social, occupation or job related.

Stress experienced by workers at work is called *Job stress* which may be due to a number of factors such as poor working conditions, excessive work load, shift work long hours at work, role ambiguity, role conflicts, and poor relationship with boss, colleagues or subordinate officers.

Reaction to stress attributed to the way the situation is perceived, the personality of the person such as the beliefs, habit, attitude and emotional responses. Certain responses indicate the presence of job stress in an individual or group. It may present itself by headache, sleep disturbance, lack of concentration, stomach upset, anxiety, short temperament, job dissatisfaction, absenteeism, low morale, and low libido in men which if not controlled may lead to erectile dysfunction causing social problem of divorce and polygamy. Also, difficulty achieving or maintaining erection can be an early signs of heart disease with coronary heart disease likely to occur two to five years after the onset of erectile dysfunction (Dr Majekodunmi, 2014). Stress could also mar one's performance (The Punch, 2014)

The physical, environmental social causes of the state are termed as *STRESSORS*. A stressor is a stimulus that places demand on an organism. To be alive is to be constantly exposed to stressors.

Cornerstone Hospital is a generational brand in health service delivery in the State. The health Centre then was opened for the use of the community on the 12thSeptember 1964 by Dr M.A. Majekodunmi.

The Health Centre has evolved from a Health Centre to become a full-fledged secondary health institution in the year 2000. The hospital was the only secondary health institution of State govern with a very wide catchment area attending to the obstetrics and gynecology at its annex located on Gbaja street approximately 1km from the hospital complex, other services includes dental, medical, pediatrics, surgical, nursing, pharmaceuticals, diagnostics and rehabilitative health care needs of the community. The hospital runs 24hours shift after this upgrading signed to a request made by Bashorun J.K. Randle on behalf of the randle family. The Governor of the State approved of the renaming of Cornerstone Hospital as a result of respect to late chief J.K. on the occasion of his post which took place on July 20 2009. The hospital is actually one of the public hospitals in the state being used as a pilot Hospital for hygiene community health programme.

PSYCHOLOGICAL WELL-BEING

Numerous recent studies have explored work stress among health care personnel in many countries. Investigators have accessed work stress among medical technicians, radiation therapists, social workers, occupational therapists, physicians and collections of health care staff across disciplines. Most of the studies focused on nurses but the studies were not always clear regarding which types of nursing personnel participated. Registered Nurses (RNs) were the dominant focus. Other investigations considered licensed Practical Nurses (LPNs) and nursing aides, licensed nurses and clerical staff.

Results of investigations have revealed effects of stress and burnout among nurses on patient outcomes. Some of these studies examined burnout in relation to increased mortality, failure to rescue and patient dissatisfaction. Similarly, in an investigation of the relationship between personal stress and clinical care, 225 physicians reported 76 incidents in which they believed patient care was adversely affected by their stress (Park et al., 2004).

Studies have shown that work is good for women's psychological well-being. Working women have lower level of anxiety and depression than non- working. Work may protect women from becoming depressed by enhancing self-esteem and increasing their social network. When the women live with very young children, however, the positive effects of work may be outweighed by role overload, role conflict and other concerns.

Research into women's work related stress in western countries has indicated a number of negative and positive factors that affect psychological well-being, high work demand, low job control, role ambiguity, inadequacy of reward, underutilization of skills, social support at work, flexible working hours, helpful supervisors, helpful colleagues and paid sick leave.

Several studies in Japan have examined the relationship between work-related stressors and psychological wellbeing in women using employees of companies and hospital nurses (Seto et al., 2004).

All the above studies show that there are stressors in hospital working environment which would not only affect the worker's health and well-being but also determine to a very high significant level their performance and the effectiveness of health care received by patients.

Also, there are large bodies of empirical evidences, suggesting that married working women faced different types of stress induced by family, job pressures and challenges.

It is therefore imperative to identify the stress factors being faced by married working women in hospitals with a view to finding the most appropriate mechanisms for managing them and to improve their productivity.

SIGNIFICANT DIFFERENCE IN THE LEVEL OF STRESS

1. There is no significant difference in the level of stress experienced by married women with different job schedules in a hospital.

2. There is no significant difference in the level of stress experienced by married women of different age, working in a hospital.

3. There is no significant difference in the level of stress experienced by married women working in a hospital based on the work experience.

This study is intended to answer the following questions:

i. Will work schedule significantly affect the stress level among married women working in hospitals?

ii. Is age difference a critical determinant of stressors suffered by married women working in hospitals?

iii. How significant is religious influence on the stress level among married women working in hospitals?

iv. Are the stressors among married women working in a hospital significantly dependent on career status?

v. Are there any significant differences in the types and levels of stress among the married women in terms of working shift or not?

FACTORS THAT IS RESPONSIBLE FOR STRESS

This study is aimed at identifying the factors that are responsible for stress within the hospital environment and to consider their effects on the married women working within such situations.

The study also investigates the perception of each group of demographic women about their job environment and also evaluates their knowledge about the type(s) of stressors associated with their schedule of duty.

The study was set out to achieve the following:

1. Identify the stress related to each job schedule or operational departments/sections in a hospital environment.
2. The impact of stress on the physiological and psychological status of married female workers in a hospital set up.

3. Assess how the respondents are coping with the stress factors in the discharge of their duties.

4. Investigate if any, the link between job satisfaction, staff morale and occupational stress.

5. Evaluate the correlation between job related stress and family imposed stress among married women working within hospital.

6. Provide suggestions as to opportunities available for the management of stress both personally and at organizational levels.

The findings of this study helped to identify the stress factors being faced by married women working in Cornerstone Hospital. It also assists in the evaluation of the management style being employed at the various managerial levels in the hospital with a view to, if need be assess those that negatively correlate to staff morale and suggest modifications.

The results of the study were used to develop health, counseling and education programmes for the concerned staff and through this enhance their performance and improve the positive perception of the patients about the staff of the hospital and the health care delivery. The study's findings could be extrapolated to other similarly run General hospitals both within the State and other parts of the country.

WORK LIMIT

The research work was limited to randomly select married women working in Cornerstone Hospital. Those to be included were selected across each operational departments and units within the hospital and also vertically along the organizational hierarchy.

DEFINITION OF OPERATIONAL TERMS

Burnout: A state of mental or physical energy depletion after a period of chronic, unrelieved job-related stress characterized sometimes by physical illness.

Hospital: An institution that provides medical, surgical or psychiatric care and treatment for the sick or the injured.

Job Satisfaction: Contentment (or lack of it) arising out of interplay of employee's positive and negative feelings towards his or her work.

Occupational Stress: Physical or psychological disorder associated with an occupational environment and manifested in symptoms such as extreme anxiety or tension or cramps, headache or digestion problems.

Perception: immediate or intuitive recognition or appreciation, as of moral, psychological or aesthetic qualities, insight, intuition, discernment.

Stress: Stress is the body's reaction to a change that requires a physical mental or emotional adjustment or response. Stress can come from any situation or thought that makes you feel frustrated, angry, nervous or anxious.

Stressor: Physical, psychological or social force that puts real or perceived demands on the body, emotions, mind or spirit of an individual.

CHAPTER TWO

THEORETICAL FRAMEWORK

Work-related stress is a pattern of reactions that occurs when workers are presented with work demands not matched to their knowledge, skills or abilities and which challenge their ability to cope. When there is a perceived imbalance between demands and environmental or personal resources, reactions may include:

- Physiological responses (for example increased heart rate, blood pressure, hyperventilation, as well as secretion of 'stress' hormones such as adrenaline and cortisol),
- Emotional responses (for example feeling nervous or irritated)
- Cognitive responses (for example, reduction or narrowing of attention and perception, forgetfulness), and behavioral reactions (for example aggressive, impulsive behaviour, making mistakes)(Maslach et al.,2001)

Stress occurs in many different circumstances, but is particularly strong when a person's ability to control demands at work is threatened. Concerns about successful performances and fear of negative consequences resulting from performance failure evoke powerful negative emotions of anxiety, anger and irritation. The experience of stress is intensified if no support or help is available from colleagues or supervisors. Therefore, social if prolonged isolation and lack of cooperation increase the risk of prolonged stress at work, as well as the negative health outcomes and increased accident risk (Houtman et al., 2007).

Conversely, work tasks with a high degree of personal control and skill variety, together with a work environment which includes supportive social relationship, can contribute positively to workers' well-being and health. When demands exceed abilities and knowledge, and the individual or the supervisor are able to perceive this, then an opportunity may arise to change this into state of balance and a challenging and motivating situation of learning and growth via discussions and actions taken by the employer and/or worker or the worker representative (Houtman et al., 2007).

OCCUPATIONAL STRESS

A difficulty in conducting stress research is that stress is defined an operationalized in many ways. For instance, the concept of stress has variously been defined as both an independent and a dependent variable, and as a process. Consequently there are numerous models and theories on stress. However, these theories are composed of the same general elements.

It is estimated that about 100 million workdays are being lost due to stress and nearly 50% to 75% disease are related to stress. Stress results in high portion of absence and loss of employment. The ratio of stress affectees in organization are increasing on alarming rate which affects both the employee performance and goal achievement (Elovainio et al., 2002).

Stress has many definitions; it is a part of both social and concrete sciences. However, stress is a universal experience in the life of each and every employee, even executives and managers. This study discloses the impact of stress on employees of organizations regardless of any discrimination of male and female employees, kind of organization and department (Bashir, 2007).

Stress is basically a mental strain from the internal or external stimulus that refrains a person to respond towards its environment in a normal manner. These stress levels can be internal or external for the doctors, from their personal lives or professional lives (Khuwaja et al., 2002). Stress is a term that refers to the sum of physical mental emotional strains or tensions on a person or felling of stress which result from interactions between people and their environment that are perceived as straining or exceeding their adaptive capacities and threatening their well-being. In addition, stress has a wide physiological and physical effect as cardiovascular, musculoskeletal systems, headache, gastrointestinal problems, sleep disturbance and depression (Imtiaz and Ahmad, 2009)

Job stress is considered as rising and has become a challenge for the employer and because high level stress results in low productivity, increased absenteeism and contributes to other employee problems like alcoholism, drug abuse, hypertension and host of cardiovascular problems (Meneze 2005)

OVERVIEW OF OCCUPATIONAL STRESSORS

Several classifications of occupational stressors exist in literature however; some of the commonest ones are:

Task related stressors: At the workplace, elements of the tasks that are carried out could be initiators of the stress process as interaction takes place with the individual. Examples of such task related stressors include issues like task complexity, task completion pace, time pressure and task ambiguity (Thompson et al., 2006).

Physical/Environmental stressors: These stressors as implied are elements of the workplace environment that are inherent to the nature of work like excessive vibration from equipment, excessive noise and heat, inadequate lighting and unavoidable exposure to weather elements (off-shore workers, fishermen, military personnel, police officers, construction, workers). Other environmental stressors include; crowding, air pollution, and toxic fumes. Administrative as well as engineering controls can be implemented to diminish most environmental/physical stressors (Wong et al., 2002).

Individual/Social stressors: These types of stressors originate from the domain of the individual or interactions with other individuals and could be objective stressors as well as perceived stressors in the workplace. Examples of individual/ social stressors can include lack of coworker support, discrimination and sexual harassment (Campbell, 2006).

Organisational stressors: These are stressors that arise from the structure of task completion processes, personal hierarchy and the environment within the workplace. Organizational stressors can also be referred to as “management stress” examples include low level of decision latitude and lack of adequate compensation (Goldenhar et al., 2003).

Occupation specific stressors: These stressors are usually characteristics of a particular profession that trigger the stress-strain process that are usually unique to that particular profession. For example; academic teaching staff may not have to experience trauma with the same frequency and duration as that of emergency response personnel, doctors, nurses, military personnel and police officers (Sobeih et al., 2006).

Safety stressors: Stressors concerning safety sometimes overlap with task related stressors like task relevance/urgency (emergency response tasks, medical emergencies) and organizational stressors like inadequate emergency training response (Wong et al., 2002).

Career and Achievement stressors: Many career and achievement related stressors were grouped as individual and organisational stressors. The reason for such classification being that sometimes, career related stressors could be perceived (ex. Feeling of limited promotion opportunities) and as such originate from the domain of the individual. Other career and achievement stressors could be objective (e.g. “the level of my ability is not being fully utilized”), and could be a result of poor organizational/managerial structure (Sui, 2002).

STRESS REACTION

The work of cannon introduced the idea that environmental pressures can cause disease rather than just short time ill effects and that people have a natural tendency to resist such forces. Cannon studied the effects of stress on animals and people and, in particular, studied the fight-or-flight reaction (the physical reaction to either fight or flight when confronted with a stressor). He saw that people react physically to stressors. When confronted with a stressor, their physiological balance changes, for example, they show increased adrenaline secretions. Cannon described these individuals as being "under stress" (Gelsema, 2007).

Hans Seyle distinguished three stages in a stress reaction in his description of the General Adaptation Syndrome (GAS). The first stage is that of an *alarm reaction*: the initial phase of lowered resistance, followed by counter shock, during which the individual's defense mechanisms become active. The second stage is that of *resistance:* maximum adaptation and, ideally, successful return to equilibrium for the individual. If adaptation mechanisms are not effective or stress continues, the individual moves to the late phase of exhaustion, where adaptive mechanisms collapse. Critique on this model has to do with simplicity. The model does not account for the fact that different stressors evoke different physical reactions. For example, anxiety producing situations are associated with adrenaline secretion, whereas aggression producing events are associated with noradrenalin secretion. Also, the GAS does not address the issue of psychological responses to stress (Copper and Driscoll, 2001).

In the 1970s and '80s stress researchers started to study the emotional responses to stress by examining burnout and emotional exhaustion. It has long been recognized that health care workers by definition are at high risk of becoming ill or burned out. Burnout is a response to the chronic stress of dealing with individuals, particularly when these individuals are troubled or having problems. When people describe themselves as experiencing burnout, they are most often referring to the experience of emotional exhaustion. Emotional exhaustion refers to feelings of being emotionally overloaded and depleted of one's emotional resources. In occupational stress research, stress reactions are often categorized into psychological, physical (health) and behavioural responses. Examples of psychological responses include anxiety and depression and burnout (Maslach, Schaufeli, and Leiter, 2001).

OCCUPATIONAL STRESS MODELS/THEORIES

Karasek's job Demand-Control Model

Karasek's demand-control model of occupational stress has had a large influcnce on the job design and occupational health literature, in part because it is quite spare, practical and testable. In Karasek's model, workplace stress is a function of how demanding a person's job is and how much control (discretion, authority or decision latitude etc.) the person has over their own responsibilities. This creates four kinds of jobs: passive, active, low strain (Jones and Bright, 2001).

Job demands represent the psychological stressors in the work environment. These include factors such as: interruption rate, time pressures, conflicting demands, reaction time required, pace of work, proportion of work performed under pressure, amount of work, degree of concentration required, and the slowing down of work caused by the need to wait for others.

Decision latitude refers to employees' control over their tasks and how those tasks are executed. It consists of both skill discretion and decision authority. Skill discretion describes the degree to which the job involves a variety of tasks, low levels of repetitiveness, occasions for creativity and opportunities to learn new things and develop special abilities. Decision authority describes both the employee's ability to make decisions about their own job, and their ability to influence their own work team and more general company policies (Hannigan et al., 2004)

Crossing the dimensions of strain and latitude gives us four stress categories for jobs, as follows:

P-High Strain Jobs (Low Latitude, High Strain): Producers are more likely to augment their strain levels by taking more on without seeking additional latitude, partly because of their appreciation of challenge and their desire to enjoy individual mastery experiences, and partly because they take an individual approach to responsibility ascription, which may cause them to overlook opportunities to ask for more latitiude. Producers enjoy levels of strain that people with other dominant styles would find excessive. Of all the styles, they are most likely to thrive in high strain jobs.

A-Passive (Low Latitude, Low Strain): As long as the passivity of a job stems from successfully forestalling disruptions, then that passivity is likely to be highly satisfying to an Administrator. Passivity that sterns from the job being either irrelevant or unimportant will not be satisfying. The Administrative style seeks to manage disruptions, by putting processes into place that cope with all contingencies and buffer the vital variables of the organization, preventing them from disruption. When latitude is reduced by following a procedure, and when that procedure causes things to proceed smoothly with low level of strain, an Administrator will take that as evidence of success. The goal state of Administration will be reached and maintaining that peace will be a pleasure.

E- Active Jobs (High latitude, High strain): Active jobs are not seen as stressful in Karasek's typology, because employees have many protective measures available to them to reduce the strain. Of all the PAEI styles, it is E that most naturally thrives in active situations. E is characterized by great ambition and almost no fear surrounding disruptions of the situations quo. Strain is thus a continual consequence of E type work. E also needs great flexibility and latitude both to stir up problems and seek out solutions. The active mode most nearly matches the mode in which E naturally works.

I-Low Strain Jobs (High Latitude, Low Strain): The combination of high levels of latitude with low levels of strain indicates that social processes are very significant in the low strain job. Employees will have a lot of authority relative to their strain levels, and thus will presumably participate more in the definition and management of tasks than in other, more stressful working environments.

The Transactional Model

The transactional model of stress and coping has been extensively researched, and at present, its theoretical underpinnings are widely accepted by researchers and practioners (Yu et al., 2007; Cooper et al., 2001). This model's central tenet is that a potentially stressful will trigger the primary appraisal process in which an individual assesses the degree of threat in relation to his or her well-being. When an event is perceived as threatening or a challenge, the secondary appraisal process provides a global assessment of the individual's coping resources and ability to manage the threat or challenge. Coping responses are initiated after the cognitive appraisals and the eventual psycho-physiological experience (stress outcomes) of this potentially stressful event depends on the effectiveness of one's cognitive appraisal stages for further actions if required.

It is worth nothing that the sequence of influence between primary appraisal and secondary appraisal does not always present itself as one being more important than the other (i.e. primary vs. secondary), or that one always precedes the other. Their relationship is far more dynamic but as a basic process. Lazarus and Folkman conceptualized a linear sequence flowing from primary to secondary appraisals to coping and eventually, to stress outcomes as a reflection of the basic pathways within the dynamic process. Therefore the key premise of Lazarus and Folkman's transactional model is that primary appraisal, secondary appraisal and coping strategies mediate the relationship between stressors and the individual's stress outcomes (Goh, 2010).

However, there is no empirical test to date on the transactional model's entire linear process with its pathway between the variables that includes stress outcomes after cognitive appraisal. The impact of cognitive appraisal on stress outcomes has been examined extensively over the past decades. Amongst the transactional theorists, Karasek elucidates this relationship succinctly; the experience of stress (stress outcomes) is a consequence of the interaction between the stressor (e.g. job demands) and the individual's perception of control over the stressor (e.g. job control). Later, the social dimension, namely social support, was added to the revised model of Job Demand-Control-Support (JDCS) (Folkman, 2008).

Theoretically, high job demand with low job control will create the successful situation. On the other hand, high job demand with high controllability will lead to an increase of motivation, skill learning and development. Although some studies have attempted to test the buffering effect of job control (and support) in the JDC(S) model, past meta-analytical study has revealed that the strain hypothesis (demands and control/ support as the additive indicators to stress) yielded more consistent support than the buffered hypothesis of the JDC(s) models. Despite numerous studies conducted with JDC(S) model, the inconsistent empirical results have led to many criticisms (Lowe and Gayle, 2007).

Research evidence of stress outcomes in the form of psycho-physiological distress preceding coping behavior is extensive in the literature (e.g. de Croon et al., 2002; Schaubroeck et al., 2001). For example Fickova (2002) reported that affectivity (positive and negative) determines the choice of coping strategy at the time of the stressful encounter.

Empirical findings that demonstrate the influence of intense emotions on the choice of coping has also been reported (e.g. Boekaerts, 2002). Although there is considerable evidence to show that coping behaviours can be influenced by stress outcomes, no empirical study is conducted to test if this relationship will remain valid within the complete transactional process as proposed by Lazarus and Folkman. This is further compounded by a lack of empirical test on the structural integrity of the basic linear sequence in the transactional process. Therefore the inclusion of another variable (i.e. stress outcomes) may alter the chronological order of the other variables, as well as the direction and number of impacts between variables within the linear sequences of the transactional process. Hence the aforementioned empirical findings on the relationships between cognitive appraisal, stress outcomes and coping behaviours remain tentative when viewed from a process prospective. Lazarus and Folkman's transactional model of stress and coping is an ideal framework to incorporate this intermediary 'stress outcomes' variable between secondary appraisal and coping.

Person-Environment (PE) Fit Theory

The PE fit literature has on the whole, been concerned with the detailed study of individuals' fit with particular aspects of their working environment and how this results in outcomes for both the person and the organization. High levels of PE fit are generally assumed to have positive outcomes (Edwards and Shipp, 2007) such as job satisfaction and commitment.

Misfit has been linked to turnover, but perhaps the most studied consequence of misfit is stress in individuals Le Fevre et al., (2003) studied PE fit and organizational stress and found that misfit increased stress levels, resulting in physiological or psychological symptoms and that misfits may employ coping or defense mechanisms in order to increase their fit. Edwards and Shipp (2007) similarly showed that the misfit between individuals' needs and what the environment supplies can lead to people experiencing stress, "such that stress exists when supplies fall short of the person's needs (Edwards and Shipp, 2007).

It has been suggested that changes in the organization cause individuals to reappraise whether they are fit (Wheeler et al., 2005), but there is no empirical evidence to show what causes people to misfit. Misfit has been shown to result in stress and low levels of job satisfaction (Jansen and Kristof-Brown, 2005) which suggests that misfits is a negative state and thus to be avoided, at least from the individual's perspective.

However, compared to the extensive work that has gone into clarifying the conceptualization of PE fit, relatively little is known about misfit. Misfit is generally assumed to be a lack of fit, where P is not equal to E (Harrison, 2007). It is known however, that sometimes, optimum effective outcomes result where there is not an exact congruence between the P and E variables (Edwards and Cable, 2009), and for example, where what is supplied by the organization exceeds what the individual needs. How misfit may be conceptualized is therefore unclear. Further, it is therefore unclear how employees experience organizational fit and misfit (Piasentin and Chapman, 2007) and whether they experience fit with different facets of the organisation simultaneously (Jansen and Kristof-Brown, 2006). One thing is clear however that "at present we know very little about the process of becoming a misfit" (Billsberry, et al., 2006). Wheeler et all (2007) concur, recognizing that "the area of misfit is wide open to researchers" and Kristof_Brown and Guay (2010) also propose misfit as a rich area for PE fit research.

Conservation of Resources Theory

Resources theories therefore offer the potential to understand the role of organizational resources in the uptake of research evidence. Resources theories are based on the premise that a minimum resource threshold is necessary for performance, with increasing difficulty arising as demands increase and outweigh the available resource pools. Resources theories have a long history and span several disciplines, including: cognitive psychology, biology, ecology, social psychology, community psychology, economics and sociology. Although researchers have adapted resource theories to understand seemingly disparate phenomena, a constant theme across all disciplines is that resources are key determinants of performance, adaptation and change (Alvaro et al., 2010).

In contrast to other resources theories, conservation of resources (COR) theory is of particular interest in understanding research use because it goes beyond merely linking resources to performance. COR theory emerged from resource and psychosocial theories of stress and human motivation. Social scientists who study stress have found that personal resources (e.g. perceived control, self-efficacy and perceptions of improvement) and social resources (e.g. emotional support, assistance from friends and family) buffer against the potential negative impact of stressful life events (Folkman and Moskowitz, 2004). COR theory extends prior theories by acknowledging that stress stems from the combined effect of the subjective perception of an event as taxing or exceeding available resources and the objective or actual environmental circumstances that threaten or cause depletion of people's resources.

Three themes of COR theory are of particular relevance in understanding limitations in capacity to using research and building the resilience for health systems change in resource-challenged environments.

Resources are required for adaptation and change

In COR theory, resources are defined objects, conditions, personal characteristicsand energies that are either themselves valued for survival, directly or indirectly, or that serve as a means of achieving these resources (Hobfill, 2000). Object resources have a physical presence (e.g. clothing, shelter). Condition resources are structures or states (e.g. status at work, good health) that allow access to or possession of other resources. Personal resources include skills and traits (e.g. occupational skills, self- esteem). Energy resources (e.g. money, knowledge) are those whose value is derived from their ability to be exchanged for other resources. It seems reasonable to predict that organizational resources may affect health systems capacity for research use in the same way that resources affect adaptation in individuals, groups, communities and organizations.

Although the concept of stages of change was not outlined in Hobfoll's COR theory, various stage based models of change suggest that some types of resources may be more important at different stages of the implementation process than others (Aspinwall, 2005)

The threat of loss leads to the protection of assets

Individuals and groups are threatened by the potential or actual loss of resources, and are therefore motivated to obtain, retain, foster, and protect valued resources for anticipated future needs. Those with fewer resources are more vulnerable to resource loss, les capable of resource gain, and highly risk-averse so they often opt to maintain existing resources rather than risk resource depletion (Alvaro et al., 2010). Research has shown that although they are generally in favour of research use individual and groups within resource-challenged health systems conserve resources for everyday and future 'rainy day' challenges (Hurst, 2007). Implementing research evidence takes resources and can have considerable implications for policy and practice. Understandably, threat can serve to increase risk aversion, to amplify resistance to change, and to limit action on research evidence.

Resources must be optimized for adaptation

According to Hobfoll, the impact of resource loss far outweighs the impact of equivalent resource gain. Nonetheless, individuals and social unit(including systems) with greater resources are often less vulnerable to resource loss, more capable of resource gain and more 'elastic' (i.e. able to take risks) than their resource-challenged counterparts. Therefore, resources must be invested to gain additional resources and to offset the potential or actual loss of resources (Hobfoll, 2000).

Although initially biased in favour of resource conservation, individuals and social units can direct themselves to enhance resources. Strategic resource investment, resource manipulation, resource mobilization (i.e. employing resources one possesses or calling upon resources available within one's environment), and resource substitutions (i.e. using specific resources in one domain to compensate for a lack of resources in another domain) are important in bolstering capacity for research use (Alvaro et al., 2010).

COR theory has recently been applied to the study of how communities cope with natural disaster and terrorism, as well as how individuals within organizations cope with occupational stress (Halbesleben, 2006).The evidence in support of COR theory as it relates to resource-challenged regions' capacity to cope with natural disaster (e.g. drought) is particularly revealing.

Resource-challenged regions continually operate in a state of depleted resources. When an external event (i.e. natural disaster) occurs, the event creates added stress on the system and causes a change in the level of resources available (Zamani et al., 2004). Still, some regions that are repeatedly affected by disaster do demonstrate remarkable resilience. Such resilience is, in part, due to proactive coping interventions aimed at buffering against the negative the negative impact of stress, such as assessing resource-related capacity to cope with stress, fostering preparedness before resources are strained, or increasing resource pools within the community or organisation.

Effort-Reward Imbalance (ERI) Model

According to the effort-reward imbalance (ERI) model by Siergrist et al., 2004, effort at work is part of a social contract that is reciprocated by adequate reward. Rewards are distributed by three transmitter systems: esteem, career opportunities and job security. Failed reciprocity between efforts and rewards may enhance the activation of the autonomic nervous system and influence the risk of coronary heart disease. According to the model, adverse health effects can also be triggered by an individual's exhaustive coping style, known as over commitment. More specifically, this model consists of three hypotheses (Bjorn, 2008):

1. The ERI hypothesis: The mismatch between high effort and low reward (no reciprocity) produces adverse health effects,

2. The over commitment hypothesis: A high level of personal commitment(over commitment) increases the risk of reduced health (even when the ERI is absent), and

3. The interaction hypothesis: Relatively higher risks of reduced health are expected in people who are characterized by conditions 1and 2.

High effort and low reward conditions have repeatedly been shown to be positively associated with the incidence of coronary events. Over commitment has also been shown to be associated with increased risks of cardiovascular disease (CVD). Corresponding support has not been found for the interaction hypothesis regarding CVD risk factors or CVD symptoms (van Vegchel, 2004).

The ERI model and its hypothesis have also been investigated in terms of self-reported health and well-being. The ERI has been found to be related to self-reported health (Godin and Kittel, 2004), poor well-being, and depression. Over commitment has been found to be associated with musculoskeletal pain, depression, psychosomatic complaints, and self-reported health in men (Bjorn, 2008).

Support for the interaction hypothesis is inconsistent. For instance, a higher risk for emotional burnout due to ERI in overcommitted employees was found in one study, but not in another (van Vegchel et al., 2001). In a comparison of results from five European studies (Belgium, France, Germany, Sweden, and the UK), variations of the components in the ERI model were reviewed according to types of occupation, education, age, and gender (Siegrist et al., 2004). In three countries, the effort scale measurements were higher in men than in women, whereas a reverse tendency was found in the UK study. Lower effort was associated with increased age in two studies with a high proportion of elderly subjects. Mean effort was significantly higher among better-educated groups in four samples, and a similar non-significant tendency was observed in a smaller German sample.

Reward did not differ according to gender in a consistent way, but there was a tendency of higher scores among older employees and especially in men. A positive association of reward with degree of education was observed in two samples. A clear cut gradient was observed with higher reward scores among higher employment grades. Men and women aged 45-54 generally had the highest over commitment scores, and employees with higher education tended to exhibit higher over commitment scores (Bjorn, 2008).

Siegrist does not specify whether the interaction hypothesis refers to additive main effects or to a synergistic effect. A synergetic understanding of an interaction effect is that the level of a moderator variable influences the relationship between the independent variables and the dependent variable. In line with such a view, we would expect the associations between effort-reward imbalance and the health variables included in this study to be strongest among employees with high scores on over commitment.

Most studies have tested for the interaction hypothesis on a variable level using regression analysis. However, because we were also interested in employees with scores on the over commitment and effort-reward scales that are supposed to have opposing effect on health (that is, the combination of low over- commitment with high effort-reward score and vice versa), we also divided the respondents into four groups according to combinations of high and low scores on the over commitment scale and the effort-reward scale, respectively. This resulted in four groups of employees: Relaxed employees, Struggling employees, Exaggerated employees, and Despaired employees.

Relaxed employees are non- over committed employees that receive sufficient reward when effort is taken into consideration. *Struggling employees* are employees that are not overcommitted, but experience an imbalance in effort compared with reward. *Exaggerated employees* are over committed employees working in an environment where effort is reciprocated with reward.

Despaired employees are overcommitted employees subjected to a working environment where their effort in work is not matched by the reward they receive. We would expect to find despaired employees to have more unfavorable scores on the health related variables compared with others. Further, we expected to find favorable health scores among *relaxed employees.* We were also interested in the groups whose scores on the over-commitment and the effort-reward scales are supposed to have opposing effects on health (that is, struggling employees and exaggerated employees).

Cognitive Activation Theory of Stress (Cats)

Physiological processes give rise to sensations registered in the brain. The interpretation of these sensations depends on the expectancies of the individual; what do they mean and what consequences will follow (Eriksen et al., 2005). Data from Ursin and colleagues demonstrate that most or all human beings experience pain from muscles, uncomfortable sensatations from the gut, and tiredness and mood changes from time to time (Eriksen and Ursin, 2002).

For some individuals, these sensations reach levels that interfere with normal life activities and quality of life to the extent that they require assistance from the health service or even hinder participation in working life. Such complaints constitute the largest source of long term sickness compensation and permanent disability in Norway, at an estimated yearly cost of between 20 and 30 billion Norwegian Kroner (National Insurance Administration, 2005).

Within the CATS framework, illness may be a consequence of sustained activation. Activation is a normal and healthy response that occurs when there is discrepancy between the value a variable should have and the real value of the same variable, i.e. a difference between what one expected and what actually happened. at work, such a discrepancy could exist between a working goal and the present situation. A discrepancy elicits an alarm reaction. For instance when an employee is faced with difficult tasks, demands or stressors, the expectancies on whether it is possible to handle the situation is important. When the individual expects to handle the situation ("positive response outcome expectancy"), the activation subsides and is not a health risk. When the individual expects to be unable to handle the situation ("negative response outcome expectancy"), the activation may be sustained with an increased risk of illness (Ursin and Eriksen, 2004).

SOURCES OF OCCUPATIONAL STRESS

Topper (2007) argued that stress is caused by unsympathetic organizational culture, poor communication between managers and employees, lack of involvement in decision-making, bullying and harassment, continual or sudden change, insufficient resources, conflicting priorities, and lack of challenges. Communication channels in the organization should be open to all employees and employee should be allowed to participate in the decision-making process of the organisation. Lack of involvement of employees by the management will make employees feel stressed.

Conflicts between home and work, and the impact on personal relationships are also contributing factors to stress (Fair brother and Warn, 2003).

The National Institute of Occupational Safety and Health (NIOSH) for example, designed a model that shows job stress and health relationships. In this model, the listed causes of stress are: physical environment, role conflict, role ambiguity, interpersonal conflict, job future ambiguity, job control, employment opportunities, quantitative work load variance in work load, responsibility for people, underutilization of abilities, cognitive demands and shift work.

Kirkcaldy, Trimpoo and Williams (2002) argued that the causes of stress include inadequate guidance and support from superiors, lack of consultation and communication, lack of encouragement from superiors, feelings of isolation, discrimination and favoritism and inadequate or poor quality training/management development. In addition other factors which are contributing to stress are; keeping up with new technologies, ideas, technology or innovations in organizations, attending meetings, lack social support by people at work and simply being visible or available.

All these stressors are related to factor management. Other causes of stress include role ambiguity, conflicting performance expectation, political climate of the organizations and poor relationship with co-workers (Manshor et al., 2003). Stress is also caused by environment demand factors and these include job content such as work load; employment conditions, such as flexible employment contracts; working conditions such as physically demanding work, and social relations at work such as mobbing expenses (Otto and Schmidt, 2007).

Factors like individual and family factors, socio-economic and financial status, mental and physical health factors contribute generally to occupational stress (Manshor et al., 2003). Harvey and Brown (2006) for instance argue that the major stressors in the workplace includes changes in technology, downsizing, sudden reorganization and unexpected changes in the work schedules, competition for promotional opportunities, lack of participation in the decision making, and lack of employee empowerment.

Others are conflicts with other employees at the workplace, inadequate time to accomplish tasks, and violence in the workplace. The issue of acts of violence in the workplace committed by both employees and customers contributes a lot to the employees stress level. Occupational stress can have grave consequences as the American Institute of Stress (AIS) indicates. Homicide is the second leading cause of fatal occupational injury and for working women it is the leading cause of death.

Silcox (2003) noted that one in five human resource managers remarked that work-related absences were growing and were in fact, their biggest problem. Moreover, research of 430 organizations by IRS Employment Review found half of the managers did not believe their employees actually sick. Human resource managers state that "workplace health has become an increasingly important part of their job, particularly when dealing with issues connected to stress" (Silcox, 2003).

Several stressors contribute to workplace stress. Those reported by the National Safety Council included the following:

- Commuting and traffic problems
- Corporate downsizing, restructuring, or job relocation
- Inability to voice concerns
- Inadequate child care
- Inadequate time to complete job responsibilities

- Inadequate training
- Keeping pace with technology
- Lack of appreciation
- Lack of clear job descriptions
- Lack of creativity and autonomy
- Poor working conditions (lighting, noise, ventilation)
- Sexual harassment and racial discrimination
- Too much responsibility with little or no authority
- Too much to do with too little resources
- Unrealistic expectations, deadlines and quotas
- Workplace violence

According to the American Psychological Association(2003), occupational stress is a multidisciplinary issue that is often difficult to measure and to identify the factors that cause it.

OCCUPATIONAL STRESSORS IN HOSPITAL WORKING ENVIRONMENT

Stressors common in health care settings include the following:

- Inadequate staffing levels
- Long work hours

- Shift work
- Role ambiguity
- Exposure to infections and hazardous substances

Stressors vary among health care occupations and even within occupations, depending on the task being performed.

In general, studies of nurses have found the following factors to be linked with stress:

- Work overload
- Time pressure
- Lack of social support at work (especially from supervisors, head nurses and higher management)
- Exposure to infectious diseases
- Needle stick injuries
- Exposure to work-related violence or threats
- Sleep deprivation
- Role ambiguity and conflict
- Understaffing
- Career development issues
- Dealing with difficult or seriously ill patients

Among physicians, the following factors are associated with stress:

- Long hours
- Excessive workload
- Dealing with death and dying
- Interpersonal conflicts with other staff
- Patient expectations
- Threat of malpractice litigation

The quality of patient care provided by a hospital may also affect health care worker stress. Beliefs about whether the institution provides high quality care may influence the perceived stress of job pressures and workload because higher quality care may be reflected in greater support and availability of resources (NIOSH, 2008).

EFFECTS OF OCCUPATIONAL STRESS

Stress sets off an alarm in the brain, which responds by preparing the body for defensive action. The nervous system is aroused and hormones are released to sharpen the senses, quicken the impulse, deepen respiration, and tense the muscles. This response (sometimes called the fight or flight response) is important because it helps us defend against threatening situations. The response is preprogrammed biologically. Everyone responds in much the same way, regardless of whether the stressful situation is at work or home.

Short-lived or infrequent episodes of stress pose little risk. But when stressful situations go unresolved, the body is kept in a constant state of activation, which increases the rate or wear and tear to biological systems. Ultimately, fatigue or damage results, and the ability of the body to repair and defend itself can become seriously compromised. As a result, the risk of the injury or disease escalates.

In the past 20 years, many studies have looked at the relationship between job stress and a variety of ailments. Mood and sleep disturbances, upset stomach and headache and disturbed relationships with family and friends are examples of stress-related problems that are quick to develop and are commonly seen in these studies. These early signs of job stress are usually easy to recognize. But the effects of job stress on chronic diseases take a long time to develop and can be influenced by many factors other than stress. Nonetheless, evidence is rapidly accumulating to suggest that stress plays an important role in several types of chronic health problems especially cardiovascular disease, musculoskeletal disorders, and psychological disorders (NIOSH, 2010).

Burnout

In many instances, the level of stress experienced on the job builds up until it is over whelming and leads to a condition called *burnout*. What is burnout?

In general, burnout is described as emotional exhaustion. The most common symptoms associated with this emotional exhaustion include overwhelming fatigue, headaches, stomachaches and impaired sleep. And, as burnout develops, it often leads to deterioration in social skills. Individuals in the midst of burnout just do not interact with others as they did in the past. They often withdraw from others. They may lose patience more easily. They may become more abrupt and abrasive in their dealings with others. Their language on job may become cruder. They may appear to be moody and depressed.

Over time, burnout has profound effects on job performance. Simply put, job performance suffers. Victims of burnout are likely to reduce the amount of work they do. They may avoid tasks that they find most stressful. Their absenteeism is likely to increase. In the worst case, they may suddenly quit their jobs with little notice to their employers. Supervisors may not be able to recognize burnout for what it is, but they certainly will notice the effects of burnout on job performance. Burnout often occurs in those jobs we think of as the helping professions. Professions such as teaching, law enforcement, nursing, and social work are all potential breeding grounds for burnout. Interestingly, within these professions, burnout tends to strike the most dedicated and most idealistic individuals.

While burnout has been observed for years in the so0called helping professions, it can occur in a wide range of jobs. The key seems to be the presence of inescapable, day-to-day frustrations which build up overtime. The frustrations that lead to burnout can take many forms. Studies of professions such as teaching and nursing have suggested that burnout occurs when workers begin to believe that no one appreciates the work they do or the help they provide. Over time the difficulty of their task and the presence of ambitious, but ambiguous, goals may lead them to believe that their efforts have no real impact. When the feeling "it doesn't matter what I do" sets in, burnout is not far behind. Of course, these feelings are not limited to the helping professions. Anytime workers feel overwhelmed by the demands of their job and think that there is little support for their efforts, burnout becomes a threat (Douglas, 2011).

Depression

Depression is a debilitating condition that places an enormous burden on society. In 2000, the World Health Organization ranked depression as the leading cause of disability worldwide (WHO, 2001). An important component of the economic impact of depression is lost productivity in the workplace. Workers suffering from depression are more likely to take time off because of short and long term disability, and depressed people tend to be less productive on the job (Goering et al., 2002)

Many studies have found that stress both on and off the job is associated with a wide variety of mental health problems. Although these relationships are not fully understood, it is thought that stress is instrumental in eroding positive self-concept, making those who experience stress more vulnerable to mental health problems such as depression. Understanding workers' vulnerability to different sources of stress is important, as is how these different stressors can interact to affect workers' mental health. Such information could help employers take steps to reduce or prevent stress, and thus perhaps lower the risk of depression (Park et al., 2004).

Depression stands out as a major occupational health issue. According to the 2002 Canadian Community Health Survey: Mental Health and Well-being, just over 1million adults aged 18 or older had experienced a major depressive episode in the year before the survey interview. More than 70% of these individuals were employed during that year. Stress on and off the job was associated with depression among workers. Men and women with jobs high in psychological demands, but with limited ability to use skills and authority to address these demands, had significantly higher rates of depression. The same was true for workers who felt a lack of support from their co-workers and supervisors, as well as for workers who generally perceived high levels of day-day stress.

However, some evidence suggests that these stressors do not occur in isolation. When the various sources of stress were considered simultaneously along with other possible confounders, the association between low supervisor support and depression did not persist for either sex, nor did the association between job strain and depression for women.

Kamel, (2008) explored the impact of occupational stress on organizational commitment among nurses in Jordanian hospitals by measuring the level of occupational stress among nurses in selected hospitals in Amman, and measuring the level of organizational commitment among them.

He found that a lower percentage of nurses with organizational commitment had sources of work stress (13.3%), compared to those with no organizational commitment (24.4%). Further, he reported that the only relation of statistical significance was between occupational stress and the department of work, p=0.03. It can be noticed that the highest percentage of nurses with occupational stress were working in specialized units (46.7%), while the least were in surgical departments (20.0%). The only relation with statistical significance was between organizational commitment and gender, p=0.01. Higher percentage of male nurses were noted among those with organizational commitment (21.7%), compare to those without organizational commitment (7.8%). No other statistically significant relation between organizational commitment and nurses' socio-demographic and job characteristics could be revealed.

The result of the study points to statistically significant positive weak to moderate correlations between sources of work stress and almost all occupational stress domains. The only exceptions were the domains of resources and workload, which were not statistically significant. Conversely, negative weak statistically significant correlations were revealed between organizational commitment scores and only three of the occupational stress domains, namely role ambiguity, work relations, and work system. It appears that total stress scores were statistically significantly and positively correlated to sources of work stress. Meanwhile, the correlation between organizational commitment scores and stress scores was negative and statistically significant.

Physical Health Effects

Stress sets of an alarm in the brain, which responds by preparing the body for defensive action. The nervous system is aroused and hormones are released to sharpen the senses, quicken the pulse, deepen respiration, and tense the muscles. This response (sometimes called the fight or flight response) is important because it helps us defend against threatening situations. The response is preprogrammed biologically. Everyone responds in much the same way, regardless of whether the stressful situation is at work or home. Short-lived or infrequent episodes of stress pose little risk. But when stressful situations go unresolved, the body is kept in a constant state of activation, which increases the rate or wear and tear to biological systems. Ultimately, fatigue or damage results, and the ability of the body to repair and defend itself can become seriously compromised. As a result, the risk of the injury or disease escalates (NIOSH, 2010).

Short Term Effects

According to the National institute for Occupational Safety and Health (NOISH), early warning signs of job stress include:

- Headache
- Sleep disturbances
- Difficulty in concentrating
- Short temper
- Job dissatisfaction
- Low morale

These symptoms interfere with an employee's sense of well-being and can result in poor health behaviors. However, they are not likely to jeopardize long- term health if stressful conditions are not sustained over a long period of time.

Long Term Effects

Chronic, sustained exposure to stressful working conditions can result in a variety of long term problems, including:

- Cardiovascular disease
- Musculoskeletal disorders

- Psychological disorders
- Workplace injury

Decades of international research has demonstrated that chronic job stress contributes to cardiovascular disease (CVD) through several mechanisms.

1) Job stress directly affects physiological processes that increase the risk for CVD:

- High cholesterol
- High blood pressure
- High blood sugar
- Weakened immune response
- High cortisol
- Changes in appetite and digestive patterns

2) Job stress contributes to behavior changes that increase the risk for CVD:

- Low physical activity levels
- Excessive coffee consumption
- Smoking
- Poor dietary habit

Consequences for the individual

The impact of distress on individuals has subjective, cognitive, physiological, behavioral and health facets to it. The subjective or intrapersonal effects of stress are feelings of anxiety, boredom, apathy, nervousness, depression, fatigue, anger, irritability and sometimes aggressive behaviors on the part of individual experiencing the stress. The cognitive effects include poor concentration, short attention span, mental blocks, and inability to make decisions. The physiological effects can be seen in increased heart and pulse rate, high blood pressure, dryness of throat, and excessive sweating. The behavioral consequences are manifest in such things as accident proneness, drinking, excessive eating, smoking, nervous laughter, impulsive behaviours, depressions and withdrawal behaviors. The manifest health effects could be stomach disorders, asthma, eczema and other psychosomatic disorders. In addition, the mental health, i.e. the ability to function effectively in one's daily life, will also decline as excessive stress is experienced (Wetzel et al., 2006).

Consequences to the Organization

Recent studies have shown that the ability of employees to manage their physiological and psychological stresses may have a significant impact on job performance (Hsieh et al., 2004). Job performance is often defined as the ability of individuals to accomplish their respective work goals, meet their expectations, achieve benchmarks or attain their organizational goals (Bohlander et al., 2001). In an occupational stress model, it has been severally observed that the ability of employees to properly control and manage their physiological and psychological stresses in performing job may lead to higher job performance in organizations (Adler et al., 2006). This finding is significant, but it has neglected to explain why effect of occupational stress on job performance is not consistent in different situations (Salovey and Mayer, 2007)

Surprisingly, a thorough review of such relationships reveals that effect of occupational stress on job performance is not consistent when emotional intelligence is present in organizations (Diggins, 2004).

Some researchers, such as Goleman (2003) and Manna et al, (2009), state that emotional intelligence (EI) has two major dimensions: interpersonal competency (how well manage ourselves) and intrapersonal competency (how well we interact with others). According to Goleman, interpersonal competency consists of three components, i.e. self-awareness, self- regulation and motivation. Interpersonal competency includes two components, i.e. empathy and social skills.

Self-awareness refers to the ability of individuals to recognize their strengths, emotions, worth and capabilities. Self-regulation is often seen as the ability of individuals to resist emotional wish (think before acting). Motivation is often related to the internal driving force that enables individuals to focus on the task at hand and continue to reach the desired goals. Empathy is frequently viewed as the ability of individuals to understand the feelings of others and this may help them to act on those feelings and meet others' need. Social skills are needed to develop and nurture good working relationships.

Relying on an organizational behavior perspective, several scholars generally conclude that El is a group of non-cognitive capabilities, competences and skills (Slaski and Cartwright, 2002), as well as a form of social intelligence where El will act as a catalyst to increase the ability of individuals to identify emotions, use emotions to guide thinking and actions, understand and manage emotions and to promote emotional and intellectual growth. If El is properly managed this may motivate employees to properly handle external demands and pressures (Lopes et al., 2006).

In the workplace stress framework, many scholars think that occupational stress, emotional intelligence and job performance are distinct constructs, but strongly interrelated.

For example, the ability of employees to properly manage their emotions and other employees' emotions will increase the ability of employees to cope with physiological and psychological stress in implementing job. As a result, it may lead to higher job performance in organizations (Gillespie et al., 2001). However, result of studies on the relationship has not shown enough evidence about the mediating effect of emotional intelligence on occupational stress (Nikolau and Tsaosis, 2002).

STRESS MANAGEMENT

Individual Stress Management

Most interventions to reduce the risk to health associated with stress in the workplace involve both individual and organizational approaches. Individual approaches include training and one-to-one psychology services-clinical, occupational, health or counseling. They should aim to change individual skills and resources and help the individual change their situation. Training helps prevent stress through (Williams et al., 2002):

- becoming aware of the signs of stress
- Using this to interrupt behaviour patterns when the stress reaction is just the beginning. Stress usually builds up gradually. The more the stress builds up, the more difficult it is to deal with
- Analyzing the situation and developing an active plan to minimize the stressors
- Learning skills of active coping and relaxation, developing a lifestyle that creates a buffer against stress
- Practicing the above in low stress situations first to maximize the chances of early success and boost self-confidence and motivation to continue.

A wide variety of training courses may help in developing active coping techniques-for example, assertiveness, communication skills, time management, problem solving, and effective management.

However, there are many sources of stress that the individual is likely to perceive outside his or her power to change, such as structure, management style or culture of the organization. It is important to note that stress management approaches that concentrate on changing the individual without changing the sources of stress are of limited effectiveness and may be counterproductive by masking these sources. For example, breathing deeply and thinking positively about a situation causing stress may make for a temporary feeling of well-being, but will allow a damaging situation to continue, causing persistent stress and probably stress to others. The primary aim of the individual approach should be to develop people's skills and confidence to change their situation, not to help them adapt to and accept a stressful situation.

Organizational Stress Management

The Organization can keep stress under control by utilizing the following means (Burke, 2002): by defining the job- by setting specific tasks, by reducing the element of danger caused by the ambiguous and conflicting function and by granting more autonomy to employees in carrying out their tasks within a well-defined organizational structure, *by setting objectives and performance standards*- the normal and achievable targets, likely to mobilize people, but without burdening the absurd tasks, *by way of sharing the burden*- careful framing of the people in positions that would match their capacities, *by way of career development*- development and promotion at work must be based on professional skills, not on an overestimation or underestimation of the employee, *through performance management*- to stimulate dialogue between managers and employees in connection with the work done, with their problems and their aspirations, *by providing advice*- creating conditions so that employees can discuss their problems with someone in service personnel, healthcare professionals of the company or in a program assistance for employees, *by training managers* in the methods of performance analysis and counseling techniques, and in terms of how to mitigate the stress affecting them but also others, by ensuring a balance between service obligations and social obligations taking up policies that take into account employees responsibilities as parents, spouses or legal guardians or providing them necessary facilitates, such as special leaves and flexible work schedules.

Organizational strategies to prevent occupational stress are quite simple; they involve the creation of a suitable working environment in terms of employment characteristics, labour relations, organizational structure and achievement of a healthy organizational culture. The *design work* must meet certain conditions to create a positive organizational climate, without stress. Positive organizational climate must allow the use of employees skill and freedom, must ensure that the loads of work are sufficiently varied and challenging to maintain interest of the employees, the tasks do not run counter their interest and that they are provided with a consistent way of working: must give employees feedback on performance obtained, take up the responsibility of the employee, enable the individual to participate in decisions concerning their own work, enable professional learning and ensure the existence of clear goals, which do not contradict the aims of others.

In terms of labour relations an important role is played by social support provided by superiors. Superiors may adopt a flexible management style, allowing employees to focus both on individual needs and on achieving the tasks of the group and making sure that the group has a spirit of cooperation. The *organizational structure* is designed in such a way as to facilitate communication within the organization. Minimizing the height of the structure, designing recipes communication to ensure communication between departments and between different hierarchical levels allows for rapid and discrete procedures of dealing with complaints and also allows for communication feedback on decision making processes, providing employees at every level with the opportunity to participate in decisions affecting their own work and future projects. In terms of *organizational culture,* positive attitude toward employees, even if there are other aspects (e.g. customers, production) considered to be priorities. Predominant focus on quality products and services essentially reflects the attention paid to employee's knowledge and skills. Mistakes are seen as opportunities for learning rather than occasions for criticism, achieving organizational goal is seen as a way of satisfying the interest of employees and personal development opportunities are available to each individual (Lazarus, 2000).

Deaconu, Podgoreanu and Rasca argue that there are three types of anti-stress strategies (Deaconu et al., 2004): primary strategies, secondary strategies and tertiary strategies.

Primary radical strategies

Primary radical strategies are very expensive and very rarely adopted, being used in cases of profound reorganization and for the purpose of a maximum reduction of ambiguity and dissatisfaction at work and cases of relocation of organizations in green places, in offices that offer all necessary facilities to reduce stress. The way of arranging the workspace (tidiness in the office, reducing the possible noise and pollution, natural lighting and appropriate temperature, decorating and maintaining cleanliness on desk, plants, ensuring adequate storage and filing, ergonomic chairs, the existence of tables for discussion, availability of service for equipment, prompt replacement of damaged equipment) should contribute to a more relaxed atmosphere.

Secondary strategies

Secondary strategies are aimed at minimizing the stress level of the organization by giving all employees access to gyms, diet treatments.

Tertiary strategies

Tertiary strategies are designed to assist people with clear signs of stress through anti-tobacco and anti-alcohol programs and confidential advice to people suffering from stress.

Organizational stress reduction measures consist of procedures of offering general and professional advice to employees. General occupational stress reduction measure refers to activities such as: reduction of work of the individual or even implementation of a program of change, simplification of procedures and of secondary tasks of different activities, enabling the individual to express unpleasant feelings about his/her condition. Professional advice made available to employees, including management team members has a significant effect in reducing organizational stress.

Companies have realized the usefulness of anti-stress programs by looking at the reduction of medical costs for their employees. The latest programs of this kind are the so-called "wellness programs" designed to take care of both the physical and psychological aspect of the employee. This may include giving up smoking and alcohol seminars, losing weight and healthy diets, exercise programs. One of such program was developed by Health Weimer Institute in California and named after an ingenious **NEW START** (also valued as a symbol) mnemo-technical formula.

The initials designate the factors considered adorable for the subjects eager to control their way of life in a direction that would prepare the body able to allow a reduction in multiple daily stressors. Thus the initials mean the following (Diener, 2000):

1. **N**- Nutrition (food),
2. **E**- Exercise(physical effort for "clearing the mind"),
3. **W**- Water (daily consumption of more than 2 litres of water),
4. **S**- Sun (sun, judicious exposure to sunlight),
5. **T**- Temperance (moderation, including periods of employment adjustment/relaxation),
6. **A**-Air (fresh air),
7. **R**- Rest (sleep and relaxation including weekends) and
8. **T**- Trust (social support, trusting somebody).

Price supported the idea that exercise, movement can reduce stress and counteract some of the adverse physiological effects, many companies introduced fitness programs for employees. Studies have shown that fitness training is associated with a better state of mind, with feeling better about oneself, reduced absenteeism and better reporting of professional performance.

EMPIRICAL STUDIES ON OCCUPATIONAL STRESS

In a study to determine the major work stressors and their impacting factors on public health nurses in Taiwan, Ho (2009) observed that among the four subscales of stressors studied, workload had the highest average stressor score and followed by managerial structure. The subscale of social role and drab work content had average scores. Of the top ten stressors, seven were in the workload area and three were in the managerial structure area. Three major stressors identified by the nurses were “diverse and complicated work content”, “heavy job responsibility” and “too much work”. The major stressors in the managerial structure area were “insufficient manpower”, “inadequate assignment from supervisor” and “unreasonable work request from superiors”. Those public health nurses who were married had significantly higher stressors than those who were not.

The analysis also showed that public health nurses who had elders to care for at home had significantly higher average scores than the nurses who did not. Years of education, job position, rurality of working district, age and number of years working as a public health nurse did not have significant difference of distribution on the workload scores.

Oubina et al., (2007) examined occupational stress among mental health professionals involving (Psychiatrists, PCH), Clinical Psychologists (CPS), as well as training staff in Psychiatry (MIR) and psychology (PIR) from different public centres in Galicia, Spain. PCH group shows stress level slightly higher than CPS group in several subscales, but differences are only significant for “identification with the patient”. The two groups coincide on the three subscales reflecting the most important stress situations, though their order is inverted for CPS group 9therapetic decisions, job criticism and deterioration and complications), compared to PCH group. Comparison of symptoms levels between the two groups showed that four (4) complaints are statistically more frequent among CPS than PCH members: Tiredness/weakness, loss of libido, abdominal pain and nausea/vomiting.

A non-parametric analysis of variance on global scores for physical complaints was made, with occupation as the independent variable. Psychiatrists are seen to be less affected by physical symptoms in comparison to the other three groups. Other variables considered in the study, such as therapeutic approach, age, experience and sex, did not show any relation to global system level. There is a trend towards higher scores on physical complaints among females than among males.

Yuriko Doi (2005) reviewed 24 studies, 13 for non-shift and 11 for shift Japanese workers, on occupational sleep research among Japanese workers identified by using MEDLINE and Japan Centra Revuo Medicina. In summary, the results reviewed are as follows. Firstly, the prevalence's of sleep problems were substantially varied among Japanese workers. Being rounded, the proportions were 5 to 29% and 29 to 38% of a symptom of insomnia for non-shift and shift workers, respectively. For non-shift workers, poor sleep quality was 33 to 44% and 42 to 45% for men and women, and excessive daytime sleepiness was 7% and 13% for men and women, respectively. Secondly, poor sleep quality was related to perceived health, sick absence, occupational activities and personal relations. Lastly, risk or associated factors of sleep problems were identified in pathophysiology (e.g., hypertension), life-style behaviours (e.g., diet, alcohol, tobacco), job- related conditions (e.g. job stress, social support, job dissatisfaction, work load, shift schedules) and psychopathology (e.g., depressed mood).

A cross-sectional study of the prevalence and associated factors of stress in 54 dental healthcare workers of an institution of higher learning in Kelantan was conducted by Rusli et al., (2006). The Malay version of the validated depression, anxiety and stress scale and Karasek's Job Content Questionnaire were used as research instruments in the study. The prevalence of stress was found to be 22.2%. One (1.9%) staff member experienced severe stress whilst 20.4% experienced mild to moderate stress. After controlling for age, sex, marital status and duration of work, psychological job demand, toxic exposures and overtime work were found to be directly associated with reported stress in dental healthcare workers. High psychological job demand, increased toxic exposures at work and increased overtime work were significantly associated with stress in dental healthcare workers.

According to data from the 2003 Canadian Community Health Survey (CCHS), nearly one in three employed Canadians, about 5.1 million, reported that most days at work were "quite" or "extremely" stressful. In 2003, health care providers comprised 6% of the Canadian work force aged 18 to 75 (data not shown). Nearly half (45%) of these workers, or 413,000, reported that most days on the job were "quite" or "extremely" stressful (hereafter referred to as "high" stress) (Wikins and Mackenzie, 2007). High work stress was reported by 42% of male health care providers and 46% of their female counterparts, a difference that was not statistically significant. However, there were differences by age. Health care providers younger than 25 were less likely to report high work stress (31%) than were those aged 25 or older. This may reflect the nature of jobs that people these ages hold, specifically, having less responsibility at younger ages. Work stress peaked at ages 35 to 54, with about 50% of health care providers in this age range reporting high work stress. The proportion fell to 41% among those aged 55 to 75.

Multivariate analysis was used to examine the relationship between the job and perceived work stress, while controlling for the effects of personal characteristics and other influences. The association between work stress and each job category was examined in separate logistic regression models that adjusted for the potentially confounding effects of day-to-day stress, life satisfaction, general health, sex and age. Even when influences outside the workplace were taken into consideration, specialist physicians, general practitioners/family physicians, and registered nurses (excluding supervisors and head nurses), had a statistically elevated likelihood of work stress relative to other health care providers. Consistent with the bivariate results, the odds ratio for nurse supervisors and head nurses also appeared to be elevated, but fell short of significance ($p=0.053$), likely because of inadequate statistical power. For medical laboratory technicians, the elevated likelihood of high work stress did not persist when other influences were controlled; suggesting that the association observed in bivariate analysis was at least partially accounted for by factors outside the job. The multivariate analysis also indicated that the odds of high work stress were significantly lower, compared with all other health care workers, for laboratory technologists, dental hygienists, and nurse aides and orderlies (Wilkins,2007).

O'Connor et al., (2000) assessed levels of mental health in General Practicioners (GPs) well after the changes in the NHIS have been implemented and included a comparable white-collar sample in order to control for socio-economic status and education level. In the study involving 1000 GPs and 400 white- collar workers in the North of England, they found that GPs were significantly more depressed and less satisfied with their job compared to the white-collar sample. Surprisingly, female GPs experienced similar levels of poor mental health and job dissatisfaction as their male counterparts. Secondly, GP's were classified according to Karasek's (1979) job strain model as 'high strain' GPs (defined as high demand & job control), 'active' GPs (high demand & high control), 'passive' GPs (low demands & low control) and 'low strain' GPs (low demand & high control).

As hypothesized, 'high strain' GPs exhibited significantly greater levels of job dissatisfaction and depressive symptoms (e.g. suicidal ideation, loss of sexual interest, feeling hopeless about the future) than all other groups, with 38% scoring equal to or above the threshold for potential clinical depression.

Burnout is common in jobs involving close contact with people, and nurses fit this criterion. Nurses in this survey reported high levels of anxiety, sleep disorders, and difficulty in handling personnel problems. In addition, nurses have more restricted social lives due to Turkish traditions and this further increased their stress.

Reported by Akgun et al., (2008) from their study of burnout among healthcare professional showed that scores obtained from all dimensions of the burnout syndrome were higher among single members of the hospital staff. The social support unit which an individual is most likely to find shelter from the conflicts and difficulties of daily life is the family. Therefore, it was expected that married individuals would report lower levels of burnout syndrome than singles.

The study also found a higher rate of burnout syndrome in the physician and nursing groups. The riskiest services provided in hospitals are those delivered by physicians to patients, so a substantial amount of stress is shouldered by doctors. This can lead to the development of burnout syndrome signs and deterioration in general health status. Although contradictory data exist in the literature, this study found a weak positive correlation between work experience and the personal success score and a weak negative correlation between work experience and the emotional burnout score. This may suggest that inexperienced staff members are more inclined to exhibit symptoms of burnout than their older, wiser colleagues. An unexpected finding was the weak positive correlation between monthly income and emotional burnout and apathy. The physician and nurse groups exhibited the highest burnout scores, yet have the highest incomes among hospital workers. A weak positive correlation also was identified between the number of daily working hours and emotional burnout and apathy. In the study carried out by llhan et al., (2005), no difference was detected between those working 40 hours per week or more and those working less. However, the study by the Turkish Medical association (2005) found that emotional burnout and apathy increased as working hours increased. The findings obtained in this study are considered an expected result.

Adebayo and Ezeanya (2010) examined how some job characteristics (job autonomy, task identity and profession) moderate the experience of burnout among health workers in Jos, Nigeria. Their findings revealed that doctors experience lower level of burnout than nurses. This does not support the findings of Uwakwe (2005) who did not find difference in the severity of burnout experienced by doctors and nurses. The present findings may be attributed to difference in their job title and in their job description. In Nigeria for instance, the job of nurses has been seen to be subordinate to that of doctors. This is what Maduakonom referred to as professional prestige and Iyang (2000) believes that is capable of enthroning professional superiority that can lead to inter-professional conflict and possibly experience of burnout. However, nursing being the subordinate profession may experience lower degree of job autonomy and task identity, thus leading to higher level of burnout.

Findings are also emerging about differences in work stress based on shift length and generational cohort. Generational differences were explored in a single-site report of 413 RNs, in which baby boomers (43 percent) and Generation Xers (41 percent) had different perceptions of work stress. The investigators expanded their work to four hospitals in the Midwest (N = 694RNs). 77 Baby boomers comprised 53 percent of the sample; their scores for stress and strain variables were significantly worse than nurses in the older and younger cohorts. The baby boomers also had significantly less social support (Cohen, Village, Ostry et al., 2004).

Lu (2008) in a study that includes a total of 246 respondents from the different wards and units at the Philippine General Hospital (PGH), majority were female (78.5%) and married (58.9%). Most of the respondents belonged to the 21-30 age group (36.18%), indicating inclusion of younger nurses. Most of the respondents had an annual income ranging from 2,000 to 3,000 USD (24.39%). Majority of the respondents have been in the nursing profession for 1-5 years (32.11%) and have employed at PGH for the same period of time (48.37%). Nurses reported that they worked impatient services (31.3%), outpatient services (10.2%), and intensive care units (ICU) (13.4%). He reported that almost half (49.6%) of the respondents reported being ill due to work in the past year, and 56.1% missed work because of an illness. It was also shown that burnout is positively correlated with organizational role stress and hazard exposure. A significant negative correlation with burnout was observed with self- efficacy, age, and situational factors, number of years working as a nurse, and sick in the last 12 months. This means that with a decrease in valuation of one-self as a nurse, burnout increases. The younger nurses who have worked lesser years were also more prone to burnout probably due to role inexperience. It was shown that age, status, number of years as a nurse, and ward assignments are significantly associated with development of burnout among nurses.

CHAPTER THREE

METHODOLOGY

This chapter focused on the methodology used for the study. The description includes the research design, setting, sample, and data collection procedures. The chapter also describes and discusses the instruments used to measure the variables and the limitations of the study.

RESEARCH DESIGN

A cross-sectional, non-experimental research design was used in this study. The design was chosen because randomization of groups was not possible. Nurses who returned a self-report survey comprised the convenience sample.

POPULATION

The populations of the study are married women working in Cornerstone Hospital and are drawn from both the operational and services or support departments of the hospital.

STUDY SAMPLE

The respondents selected were married women within the ages of 25 and through stratified random sampling from various departments of Cornerstone Hospital. These include Nurses, Administrative officers, Pharmacists, Health Attendants, Medical

Record Officers, Catering and Medical Laboratory officers, the respondents. The study sample includes personnel at different career levels and only those who have more than one year experience in the study setting. These criteria were chosen because the respondents would be well-oriented to the organization past the initial stress of working in a new environment, as experienced by part time employment.

INSTRUMENT OF DATA COLLECTION

A self-administered questionnaire was used for collecting data for this study. The questionnaire was developed by the researcher based on pertinent literature search. It consisted of two sections demographic data and measurement of occupational stressors. The second section is based on a

Four 4 point Liker Scale scored as follows;

Strongly Agreed	4 points
Agreed	3 points
Disagreed	2 points
Strongly Disagreed	1 point

INSTRUMENT VALIDITY

The questionnaire was presented to my project Supervisor for evaluation, criticism and modification. The corrected and approved questionnaire was then administered on respondent.

RELIABILITY TEST

After review of the questionnaire by experts and its approval, two pilot studies were carried out twice in three weeks interval before starting the actual data collection. The purpose of the pilot studies was to ascertain the clarity, and applicability of the study tools, and to identify the obstacles and problems that may be encountered during data collection. It also helped to estimate the time needed to fill in the questionnaire. Based on the results of the pilot study ,modifications, clarifications, omissions, and rearrangement of some questions were done. It was done on 20 nursing personnel working in different units, and these were not included in the total sample of the research work to ensure stability of the answers.

The result of the two pilot studies was compared for agreements using Pearson's Product Moment Correlation. The co-efficient of correction, r = 0.983 obtained shows that the two set of results are highly correlated. This means that the instrument as developed is reliable and compatible for the study.

METHODS OF DATA ANALYSIS

The average values obtained by each demographic group under each of the sections of the questionnaire were presented in frequency tables for a vivid analysis and comparison of the level and pattern of stress among the groups as well as the coping capacity.

Hypothesis 1 – 3 were tested using Chi- Square(X^2) analytical tool, The calculated Chi- Square values were compared with the corresponding values from statistical table for significance test at 95% confidence level.

$X^2cal=\sum [(E - O)^2 / E]$

$E= (Cij \times Rij) / T_{tot}$

Where:

E : Expected values

O: Observe value

C: Column total of observed values

R: Row total of observed value

T_{tot} :Total of all values

ETHICAL CONSIDERATION

Before any attempt to collect data, two formal letters were written to the Management of the Hospital to obtain an official approval for the conduct of the study. The letters identified the researcher, the title and aim of the research. The confidentiality and ambiguity of the respondents were assured and ensured by not including data request that can be used to identify the respondents. Likewise, the questionnaires were collected randomly as they are been filled and not according to department.

CHAPTER FOUR

CONCLUSION AND RECOMMENDATION

This study considered the sources of stressors faced by married women working in Randle General Hospital, Surulere, Lagos State. Data collected revealed certain critical information with implications for both the personnel and management of the hospital, as a typology of its kind. The result also identified knowledge gap that would need to be covered in further studies.

CONCLUSION

After due analysis of the results of the study, the following conclusions are made:

i. Respondents are exposed to some common stressors which are positively correlated with their job.

ii. The management and superior personnel showed good management practices in terms of communication, consultation, encouragement and support.

iii. The office politics as source of stress cuts across all cadre and departments studied.

iv. The differences in stress faced by respondents on the basis of age, job schedule and present years of job experience show statistical significance.

IMPLICATIONS OF THE STUDY

The study revealed that married women in the hospital irrespective of department, work experience, age and educational status face varying levels of stress occasioned by exposure by their job routines. Some positive management practices were shown such as support by superiors, good communication as well as encouragement by superiors.

RECOMMENDATIONS

In view of the findings of the study, the following recommendations are made:

i. The management should device mechanisms to reduce work load by the staff.

ii. Organise periodic stress management seminars and workshops for staff of the hospital.

iii. Improvement in the social supporting system within the structure of the hospital should be considered.

iv. The personnel should be made to undergo stress test at intervals.

SUGGESTIONS FOR FURTHER STUDIES

Only married women were covered under the present study, there is the need to conduct further studies covering all the staff irrespective of gender or marital status. Likewise empirical studies that will quantitatively determine the stress level in relation to prevalence of hypertension (systolic and diastolic) among hospital staff should be conducted. This study can be replicated in other hospitals- private/public, federal state, local government, primary, secondary and tertiary hospitals.

REFERENCES

Adebayo S.O and Ezeanya I.D (2010).Effects of Job Autonomy.Task identity and Profession on Burnout among Health workers in Jos, Nigeria.

European Journal of social sciences 14 (1): 116-124

Adler D.A, McLaughlin T.J., Rogers W.H., Chang H., Lapitsky L., Lerner D. (2006) Job performance deficits due to depression.

The American Journal of Psychiatry, 163:1569-1576

Akinboye J.O, Akinboye D.O and Adeyemo D.A. (2002) Coping with Stress in Life and Work place. Ibadan: Stirling-Horden Publishers (Nig) Ltd.

Akugun Seval, Al- Assaf A.F. and BakanCoskun (2008) Reducing burnout among hospital professionals: EAPa can help identify and alleviate the factors that cause burnout and improve the health and performance of hospital staff. The Journal of Employee Assistance; ISSN 1544-0803.

Albar Marin M. J. and Garcia-Ramirez (2005) 'Social Support and Emotional Exhaustion among Hospital Nursing Staff'. European Journal of Psychiatry; 19(2): 96-106.

Al-Fadli, F.S. (1999) The relationship between clarity of organizational goals, role ambiguity, role conflict and job stress: Case of the Public sector in Kuwait. Journal of King Saud University: Admin Sciences; 11 (2): 135-170.

Bashir Asad (2007) Employees' Stress and Its impact on their performance, First proceedings of International Conference on Business and Technology, December 17, 2007, Pages 156-161. Iqra University Islamabad.

Boekaerts M. 2002 Intensity of Emotions, emotional regulation and goal framing: how are they related to adolescents' choice of coping strategies? Anxiety, Stress and coping; 15: 401-412.

Campbell F. (2006) Occupational Stress in the construction industry. Berkshire, UK: Chartered Institute of Building.

Copper C.L., Dewe P.J and O'Driscoll M.P. (2001) Organizational Stress: A review and critique theory, research and application (pp. 159- 183, pp. 233-252). Thousand Oaks: Saga Publication, Inc.

Edward S.J.R and Shipp A.J (2007).The Relationship between person- environment fit and outcomes.

Elovainio M., Kivimaki M. and Vahtera J. (2002) Organizational justice: evidence of a new psychosocial predictor of health. American journal of Public Health; 92(1): 105-108

Fickova E. (2002) Impact of negative emotionality on coping with stress in adolescents.StudiaPsychologica; 44: 219-226.

Folkman S. (2008) the case for positive emotions in the stress process. Anxiety, Stress and Coping, 21 (1), 3-14.

Follcman, S (2008). The case for positive emotions in the stress process. Anxiety, stress and Coping 21(1), 3-14.

Gelesema Tanya Irene (2007) Job Stress in the Nursing Profession. Doctoral Dissertation, Leiden University, ISBN 978-90-9021917-2.

Gelsema Tanya Irene (2007). Job stress in the Nursing profession. Doctinal Dissertion, Leiden University ISBN 978-90-9021917-2

Goh Y.W. Sawang S and Oei T.P.S (2010). The Reviseed Transactional Model (RTM) of occupational stress and Coping. An improved process approach.

Goh Y.W., Sawang S., and Oei T.P.S (2010) The Revised Transactional Model (RTM) of Occupational Stress and Coping: An improved process approach. The Australian and New Zealand journal of organisational Psychology; 3: 13- 20.

Goldenhar L., Williams, L. and Swanson N. (2003) Modelling the relationship between job stressors, injury and near-miss outcomes for construction labourers. Work and Stress; 17(3): 218-240.

Hannigan B., Edwards D., and Burnard, P. (2004) Stress and Stress management in clinical psychology: Findings from a systematic review Journal of Mental Health, 13(3), 235-245.

Houtman Irene, Jettinghoff Karin and Leonor Cedillo (2007) Raising awareness of stress at work 6 by World Health Organization, 20 Avenue Appia, 1211 Geneva 27, Switzerland.

http://www.athealth.com/consumer/disorders/workstress:html

Imitiaz Subha and Ahmad Shakil (2009) Impact of stress on employee productivity, performance and turnover; an important managerial issue.

International Review of Business Research Papers; 5(4): 468-477.

Jones, F., and Bright, J. (2001) Stress: Myth, theory and research. London: Prentice Hall.

Lattore Mdo. R and Cooper S.P (2005). Job Control, Job demands, Social supports at work and health among adolescent workers. Rev Sande Public 39. 245-253.

Lowe J., and Gayle, V. (2007) Exploring the work/life/study balance: the experience of higher education students in a Scottish further education college. Journal of Further and Higher Education, 31 (3), 225-238.

Maslach, C., Schaufeli, W.B. and Leiter, M.P. (2001).Job burnout. Annual Review of Psychology; 52: 397-422.

Meneze M.M. (2005) The Impact of Stress on productivity at Education Training and Development Practices: Sector Education and Training Authority.

National Institute for Occupational Safety and Health (2008).Exposure to stress occupational hazards in Hospitals. U.S Department of Health and Human Services (NIOSH) Publication No. 2008-136

Omolayo Bunmi and Mokuola Bola (2008). Influence of Percieved Job Tension on stress reaction among Hospital and University workers in Nigeria. Bangladish Journal of Scientific Industrial Research; 43 (3) 353-358.

Park K.O, Wilson M.G, Lee M.S. (2004) Effects of social support at work on depression and organizational productivity. American Journal of Health Behaviour; 28(5):44-55

Rusli B. N., Edimansyah B. A. and Naing L (2006). Prevalence and associated factors of stress in dental healthcare workers of a higher Institution of learning in Kelantan. Archieves of Orofacial Sciences; 1:51-56.

Seto Masako, Morimoto Kanehisa and Maruyama Soichiro (2004) Effects of work related factors and work- family conflict on depression among Japanese working women living with young children. Enviromental Health and Preventive Medicine; 9: 220-227

Sobeih T., Salem O. Daraiseh N., Genaidy A. and Shell R. (2006) Psychosocial factors and musculoskeletal disorders in the construction industry: a systematic review. Theoretical Issues in Egronomics; 7(3): 329-344.

Thompson B., Kirk A. and Brown D. (2006) Sources of stress in policewomen: A three-factor model. International Journal of Stress management; 13 (3): 309-328.

Topper E. F. (2007) Stress in the Library. Journal of New Library 108(11/12): 561-564.

Ursin H. and Eriksen H. R. (2004) The cognitive activation theory of stress. Psychoneuroendocrinlogy ; 29(5):567-592.

Van Vegchel N., de Jonge J., Meijer T., and J.P. (2001) Different effort constructs and effort reward imbalance: Effects on Employee well-being in health care workers. Journal of Advanced Nursing; 34(1):128-136.

Wilkins Kathryn (2007) work stress among health care provider. Health Reports (Statistics Canada, Catalogue 82-003) 18 (4): 33-36.

Wong T., Chen W., Yu S., Lin Y., and Cooper C. (2002). Percieved sources of occupational stress among chinese off-shore oil installation workers. Stress and Health; 18: 217-226.

Yu L., Chiu, C.-H., Lin, Y-S., Wang Chen, J.W. (2007) Testing a model of stress and health using meta-analysis. Journal of Nursing Research, 15(3): 202- 214.

Zamani G. H., Gorgievski-Duijvesteijn M. J. and Zarafshani K. (2004) Coping with drought: towards a multilevel understanding based on conservation of resources theory. Health. Human Ecology, 34:677-692.

www.ingramcontent.com/pod-product-compliance
Lightning Source LLC
LaVergne TN
LVHW050334160826
845677LV00014B/3619

* 9 7 9 8 3 5 2 8 9 1 5 7 5 *